A Daughter's Journey

Walking with God as a Woman of God

A Daughter's Journey

Walking with God as a Woman of God

Natalie Jones

ABUNDANT HARVEST
PUBLISHING

A Daughter's Journey
Copyright © 2020 by Natalie Jones

ALL RIGHTS RESERVED
No portion of this book may be reproduced, stored in any
retrieval system, or transmitted in any form or by any means,
electronic, mechanical, photocopy, recording or otherwise,
without the express written consent of the author.

Editing/Formatting: McKenna Hafner and Erik V. Sahakian
Cover Design/Layout: Andrew Enos

All Scripture is taken from the New King James Version of the
Bible. Copyright © 1979, 1980, 1982 by Thomas Nelson, Inc.
Used by permission. All rights reserved.

Library of Congress Control Number: 2020907862

ISBN 978-1-7349949-0-2
First Printing: June 2020

FOR INFORMATION CONTACT:

Abundant Harvest Publishing
35145 Oak Glen Rd
Yucaipa, CA 92399
www.abundantharvestpublishing.com

Printed in the United States of America

This book is dedicated to my husband and mom, who have both supported and believed in what God is doing with this message.

Contents

Introduction ……………………………………………...11

1. Choosing Your Path …………………………………15

2. Becoming Daddy's Little Girl …………………………31

3. Holding Daddy's Hand ………..................................43

4. Daddy, Carry Me ……………………………………..57

5. The Boy in the Sandbox ………………………………67

6. Don't Let Go ……………………………………………77

7. Patience, Little One …………………………………...85

8. Daddy, Who is He? ……………………………………...89

At that time the disciples came to Jesus, saying, "Who then is greatest in the kingdom of heaven?" Then Jesus called a little child to Him, set him in the midst of them, and said, "Assuredly, I say to you, unless you are converted and become as little children, you will by no means enter the kingdom of heaven. Therefore whoever humbles himself as this little child is the greatest in the kingdom of heaven."

Matthew 18:1-4

Introduction

When I started writing this book ten years ago, I had the vision of and ambition for a simple message to all young girls. That message was simple and enormous, yet sweet enough to imagine and challenging enough to see value at the same time. In a world that idolizes beauty and perfection, young women are opened to a constant struggle with direction and guidance.

As you read this book, you will find that the majority of the content is presented in an imaginary realm—a painted picture of a father and his young daughter walking side-by-side down a path that represents life. As they encounter events and obstacles along the way, the metaphorical scenario is translated into the problems and situations we face in everyday life.

When Jesus said to have faith like a child in Matthew 18, what did He mean? And, to go along with that question, what does it mean when you are asked, "How is your walk with God going?" We hear these truths and questions, but we struggle to really comprehend what it means to have faith so pure as to liken it to a child. We have a hard time living life with that perspective. Living such a life with obedience to purity requires a dose of faith.

If you have ever spent time with children, you know that they basically have no concept of the fear of failure. They also have no sense of personal space! They say whatever comes to mind, which can often be brutally honest at times. Yet that's the image Jesus gave us when the children were all gathering around Him. Receiving the kingdom of God like a child is one thing. Having a childlike faith (unhindered and pure) is something completely different. That is a quality that we need to understand better.

Everything is new for a child. Because of that, they venture forward with a heart and attitude that isn't tainted or jaded by past experience. Unfortunately, as time moves on and they get older, past experience attaches a tether to a person each time failure takes place. Those tethers are anchored deep by fear and disappointment. This inevitably gives way to hesitation and skepticism.

We are faced with choices and challenges every day. We must grasp the understanding that God is a loving Father who walks alongside us as we face those challenges. Such an understanding can change our entire perspective. As we trust Him with our whole heart and let go of past mistakes and seemingly insurmountable disappointment, we can walk forward with the knowledge that our Daddy is holding our hand. We know that He will never leave us nor forsake us.

The challenges that young women face today are quite unique in that those distractions and contradictions come from all different angles—especially with the increasing popularity of social media. This is the reason why I want to paint the picture of a young girl walking hand-in-hand with her Daddy. As she keeps her eyes on him, she no longer notices the distractions and temptations of this world. Another desire is often revealed and met, too…there is a boy walking alongside her and her Daddy.

1

Choosing Your Path

Should I get a small drink or a large drink? Should I buy the black pants or the regular jeans? Should I start my project today or tomorrow (after all, I have a whole two weeks to finish it…)? Whether they are important or insignificant, we are forced to make decisions every single day. Most of the time we make decisions without even thinking twice about the consequences because, well, they're not really going to affect anything in such an immense manner as to change the course and direction of our lives. So we make the decision to buy the large soda and the black pants, and we leave our school projects to be finished the day before they're due. But what about the really big decisions, like what am I going to do with my life after I finish high school? Or even smaller decisions that you don't think can affect your life drastically, such as should I go to the party? Should I hang out with those friends even though they do drugs? Should I go out with that cute guy who asked me out today?

You may be thinking that those choices aren't that big of a deal or that they won't have any real consequences. The truth is…they absolutely do! It may be a whole lot of fun to go to that party and get hammered, or to go all the way with your boyfriend, or to do something thrilling like sneaking out late to do drugs with your friends, but in the end you will still feel an emptiness in your heart. Nothing you ever do will fill it. The only one who can fill it is the very one who created it—Jesus Christ.

God uniquely designed your heart in a way that left a place for Him. No person or thing can ever take that place from Him. Jesus Christ gave His life on the cross so that you can choose to follow Him and have the assurance of eternal life. Jesus said in Mathew 10:38-39, "And he who does not take his cross and follow after Me is not worthy of Me. He who finds his life will lose it, and he who loses his life for My sake will find it." In other words, Jesus is telling you to surrender your life over to Him. You need to die to yourself and give up the driver's seat to Him. When we do this, we won't regret it. When you give your life to Jesus, He will make your plans better than you could ever dream.

I want you to picture yourself standing in the middle of nowhere. Then add some scenery to your setting. Tall, lush trees. Beautiful, yellow tulips. Thick, green grass—greener than the most vibrant colored frog you've ever seen. Now, beneath your feet and in front of you, add a dirt road that looks as though it's been carved by human hands. That's your life's path.

Throughout your life, you've walked alone along this path, unsure of the direction you're going. Seemingly out of nowhere, you come across a split in the road. You stop to ponder which way to go (which you've never done before because before you would only think of your own selfish desires, instead of being concerned about the consequences of your decisions). Which way do I go? Should I drink alcohol, do drugs, and use foul language just so I can fit in with the "cool" crowd? Or do I choose to live my life for a love that's higher than my own? Close your eyes and picture the road that Jesus is on and the road He isn't on. Then choose.

Making decisions is an inescapable part of life. Whenever you have a hard time making a decision (whether big or small), look at the path you're taking and ask one question. Is Jesus on it? Matthew 7:13-14 says, "Enter by the narrow gate; for wide is the gate and broad is the way that leads to destruction, and there are many who go in by it. Because narrow is the gate and difficult is the way which leads to life, and there are few who find it." It won't always be a piece of cake walking down your path with Jesus, but it's a million times better than walking it alone.

Now that you've established your path and understand that Jesus is with you at all times (Matthew 28:20; Hebrews 13:5-6) no matter what happens, your path may develop little pebbles. Those pebbles may eventually mature into rocks. Pretty soon you find yourself constantly watching your step because the rocks have covered the road that you could once see so clearly. However, you look over and find that the rocks haven't taken up the whole road like you thought. Just a few steps to your left and you would be out of the forest of sharp, overgrown pebbles.

You haven't fallen yet and that's exciting. You feel invincible, untouchable. You're living on the dangerous side by being a little daring. You're still walking with Jesus, but you're also doing your own thing. You've given your life to Jesus, but you still listen to foul music on the radio and watch perverse music videos on MTV. You still hang out with your old friends, and not a day goes by that you're not pressured to go back to your old lifestyle that you loved.

You still have the urge to go with those friends and get totally wasted, so after a few threats of abandonment, you give in. You have a whole lot of fun and remember the excitement, pleasure, and satisfaction of your old life. You remember how you used to dress that would get boys to look at you in a lustful way. Eventually, you're back to caring less about what your parents say and disrespecting them. Before you know it, you're right back to doing the things you told yourself you'd stop doing.

You're quickly caught in between two worlds. The old life on one hand and your life with Christ on the other. You have the assurance of the commitment you made to the Lord, but you're also still enjoying the perverseness of the world. Since you haven't got hurt yet, you feel unstoppable. You don't understand the dangerous position you are in.

You get so comfortable in this middle ground that after some time you stop paying attention to how you are walking altogether. You haven't fallen yet and don't think you ever could. You can manage yourself, after all. It's once you've become immune to the fact that you're walking among razor sharp rocks that you lose your footing. Your foot becomes trapped by an unseen groove in a rock and your body plummets down to an ocean of rough, ragged, unforgiving rocks.

The pain is unbearable. You struggle to free your foot, but the cranny has imprisoned it. Every move you make causes more pain to the injured foot. You've scraped up both your hands and your knees. Nothing you do helps; you're stuck and it was your own fault for walking so carelessly.

Now that you're down, you hear the whispers of the devil blaming you for falling into the trap he set for you.

The trap was the luring appearance of the rocks. They didn't appear to be harmful. In fact, they looked fun and exciting! Of course they appeared that way. Do you think the devil would make sin look like it wasn't fun? That's how he traps you—with enticing temptation. He tells us, "It's not bad to listen to that music. It's not going to hurt anyone if you watch pornography. It's not a big sin to smoke that joint. Show off the body your mama gave you. Sleep with your boyfriend, you won't get pregnant."

These thoughts pop into your head and you convince yourself that it's not that big of a deal to follow through with the idea. You listen, you fall, and then the devil laughs at you for being gullible, ignorant, and hypocritical. He won't quit drilling those thoughts into your mind. He won't give up until you are completely discouraged. He wants to bring you to the point where there is nothing anyone can say that will make you feel better. To the point where you believe that no one will understand quite how badly you've sinned against God.

Yet there is hope…God forgives! No matter how many times you sin, He will forgive you as long as you admit that you have sinned. In Proverbs 28:13, Solomon (the son of King David) wrote, "He who covers his sins will not prosper, but whoever confesses and forsakes them will have mercy."

You may even try to cover up your sins, but God still sees them. Jeremiah 2:22 tells us, "'For though you wash yourself with lye, and use much soap, yet your iniquity is marked before Me,' says the Lord God." There's no point in trying to destroy the evidence of your sinfulness. You may succeed in hiding it from the people around you, but not from God. God will forgive you; He has promised that in His Word. Don't fall into the trap of believing that what you've done is too dark or unforgiveable. Remember what it says in Romans 8:1, "There is therefore now no condemnation to those who are in Christ Jesus…"

Reach out your hand to Him and Jesus will pull you out of the rocks. He is always there to help you when you ask Him to. After He helps, don't put yourself in that situation again. Avoid going places and doing things that have even the slightest possibility of temptation. It is not a sin to look at the rocks on your path; however, it is a sin to go walk on them.

Once you're aware of the rocks on your path and know how to avoid them, you feel a little bit more confident with your direction. The sun is shining, giving off a warm glow to your path. The birds are chirping as they float past you gathering food. There's a steady cool breeze kissing your cheeks. You're enjoying the scenery so much that you don't even realize that your little dirt road has started to grow small spurts of grass. It's not a drastic change to your path, so you don't notice it very much. But after some time, the grass gets thicker and thicker. It grows all the way to the point where you can hardly see your path at all anymore. You're stuck! How can you be sure exactly where to go?

There are some situations in life that make you feel very unsure and nervous. It could be anything from a bad math grade, to an upcoming graduation, to your friendships, or even a potential job. You can't see a clear picture and that makes you nervous. You feel lost and scared. How do you know the outcome? Should you say yes or no? Do you even have the option to give a yes or no answer? You've stopped in the middle of your unclear path; the road ahead becomes hazy.

The story of Ruth in the Bible describes the life of a young woman whose path became unclear without warning. Ruth, a Moabite, had married an Israelite, one of the widow Naomi's two sons. Though she didn't believe in the God of Israel, she was joined to a man who did. After ten years of marriage and living in Moab, Ruth's husband and his brother both died. This left Naomi with two daughters-in-law and no husband or sons.

Unsure of what to do, Naomi took Ruth and Orpah (the second daughter-in-law) and began the journey back to

Judah. Along the way, the two young widows were told that they could return to their own mothers. Orpah went back, but Ruth stayed with Naomi. Ruth's decision confused Naomi and so the mother-in-law encouraged her remaining daughter-in-law to follow Orpah's suit. Ruth, however, answered Naomi in Ruth 1:16, saying, "Entreat me not to leave you, or to turn back from following after you; for wherever you go, I will go; and wherever you lodge, I will lodge; your people shall be my people, and your God, my God." Instead of running back to the gods of her people, Ruth chose to follow the God of Israel who Naomi worshiped. She chose to follow God and stayed loyal to her mother-in-law, not knowing the outcome of her decision.

So Naomi and Ruth went to Bethlehem at the beginning of the harvest. It was there where Ruth offered to glean the fields after the reapers. Because of her hard work, she caught the attention of one of the landowners named Boaz. He was a kinsman of Elimelech, her father-in-law. It was because of her work ethic that Ruth found favor in Boaz's eyes.

After some time, Boaz married Ruth and she gave birth to a son named Obed, and to Obed was born Jesse, the father of David. Ruth was the great grandmother of King David, the giant slayer in First Samuel 17. Ruth was even mentioned in the genealogy of Jesus in Matthew 1. How crazy is that! Though she was given the option to return to her old life, she chose to follow the God of Israel. For that, she was immensely rewarded.

God has a plan for your life too! Though it may not be clear right now for you, He can see the big picture. Don't be afraid; follow Jesus. He always knows the way, even when it's too thick for you to see where you're going. Have faith that Jesus will take care of you and stop trying to find a way through the tall grass yourself. You will only get more lost and confused. I know it's frightening to let someone other than yourself lead, but that's what we must do.

You may be thinking, *How do I let Him lead me if He's not here telling me what and where to go?* The way you let Him lead is through prayer. Talk to God and ask Him to take over those problem areas in your life. When you surrender the wheel of your life to God, He will never let you down. He just requires you to first let go. In Matthew 6:33, Jesus says, "But seek first the kingdom of God and His righteousness, and all these things shall be added to you." If God is first in your life, then everything else will fall into place. It's only when you put Him first that He can have complete control of your situations, your problems, and your blessings.

Finally, your path clears. You doubted for so long whether or not Jesus could lead you through such uncertainty, but now you're in the clear and believe the worst is over. What else could happen? Your comfortability leads you to let your guard down and lose track that Jesus is still with you, so you return back to your old life again. You go back to listening to the wrong music, you stop listening to your parents, and you decide to watch R-rated movies again.

The grass has cleared and you believe you don't need to be obedient to God anymore. You're back on the right track and everything is great. But as you're walking, you see clouds looming on the horizon. It looks like a storm, but you ignore it, thinking it'll pass.

However, the bright and shining sun is soon concealed behind dark, unforgiving clouds. The wind and rain hit you like a ton of bricks. The once magnificent scenery of your path is transformed into a minefield. Trees break from the forceful wind and come tumbling down in front of you with a loud crash. It's frighteningly dark. You're cold and wet. Lightning flashes as thunder simultaneously snaps your eardrums. The wind howls and scrapes against your face. You feel so alone and helpless against such a powerful storm. Is there anyone that can protect you from the storm? Does anyone care to come and rescue you?

There are situations in life that present themselves and make you feel like you've just got caught in a category 5 hurricane. Perhaps a death in the family, or your best friend moves away, or you're caught doing drugs at school, or your school counselor informs you that your grades are too bad for you to graduate. These are things that come unexpectedly and put a huge caution with flashing lights right in the middle of your path. It's too late for you to go back; you made the decision and it has drastically changed the condition of your path. The problems are overwhelming and never seem to go away. You can't run away. Everything you do reminds you of them. The sinking feeling in your gut never diminishes. Your fear is so great that you forget you're not alone. You forget that Jesus is right next to you, waiting for you to give up trying to fight the storm yourself. He's waiting for you to give Him control over the situation.

Jesus' disciples faced a similar situation in Matthew 8:23-27. They were with Jesus out at sea when a great storm took over their boat. Verse 24 tells us that the boat was covered with waves, but as the storm raged, Jesus slept. The disciples were so terrified that they awoke Him and said, "Lord, save us! We are perishing!" (Matthew 8:25). This is exactly what God wanted the men to do—call for Him. He will not force Himself upon you if you do not ask for His help. He has the power to control whatever situation comes your way, but He is waiting for you to relinquish control. If everything was always sunny and easy on our path, we wouldn't need God. Sometimes storms arise to teach us that we desperately need Him.

After the disciples called out to Him, Jesus answered, "Why are you fearful, O you of little faith?" (Matthew 8:26). Afterward, Jesus rebuked the winds and the sea, and there was calm. Jesus has the ability to calm a storm at any time. We must have the faith that this is so. That is the point of this biblical narrative. Jesus has the power to control anything and everything. The disciples knew this, but fear clouded their judgment. They neglected to remember that Jesus was in the boat with them. They needed to trust Him and have the faith to believe that Jesus would save them from drowning.

There is a second incident in Matthew where the same idea is demonstrated. After Jesus fed the five thousand, He sent His disciples ahead of Him to cross the sea while He spent time alone in prayer. Their boat was again overcome by a storm. This time, however, Jesus was not physically with them on the boat. Matthew 14:25-27 says, "Now in the fourth watch of the night Jesus went to them, walking on the sea. And when the disciples saw Him walking on the sea, they were troubled, saying, 'It's a ghost!' And they cried out for fear. But immediately Jesus spoke to them, saying, 'Be of good cheer! It is I; do not be afraid.'" There are so many times in life when we are tempted to jump to conclusions and give credit to someone else instead of to God. Instead of remaining calm, we freak out just like the disciples did. They believed Jesus to be a ghost, instead of their Lord coming to save them.

Jesus called out to His disciples to not be afraid. It was then that the men realized it was not a ghost, but Jesus Christ Himself. Peter then called out to Him and Jesus commanded him to walk out onto the water. Matthew 14:30-31 says of Peter, "But when he saw that the wind was boisterous, he was afraid; and beginning to sink he cried out, saying, 'Lord, save me!' And immediately Jesus stretched out His hand and caught him, and said to him, 'O you of little faith, why did you doubt?'" Most of the time we start our walks out strong, believing and trusting in Jesus. However, our fear of the severity of our problems causes us to take our eyes off Jesus. The moment we look away we start to feel like we are sinking. Take notice of Matthew 14. When Peter started to sink, he called out for Jesus to save him and Jesus immediately pulled him out. Jesus will never hesitate to save you; you just need to call out to Him.

It is important that you never doubt the strength of God's power. He is capable of pulling you out of any situation as long as you allow Him to. He has sovereignty over nature, over the wind, over the waves and currents, over all things. Only Jesus can calm the storms of your life. Do not forget that even though the storm is big, Jesus is bigger. It is for this reason God tells Joshua, "Have I not commanded you? Be strong and of good courage; do not be afraid, nor be dismayed, for the Lord your God is with you wherever you go" (Joshua 1:9).

Don't view the storms of your life as a time to be afraid, but rather as a time to examine yourself. These hindrances aren't always a bad thing. God allows these storms to come onto our path so as to test you. He wants to know whether you will run to Him or away from Him. The book of James describes these times as an opportunity to learn. James writes, "My brethren, count it all joy when you fall into various trials, knowing that the testing of your faith produces patience. But let patience have its perfect work, that you may be perfect and complete, lacking nothing" (James 1:2-4).

Allow the storms to make you stronger. Let them teach you a lesson that you would've not been taught otherwise. Look up to your heavenly Daddy and learn to dance with Him in the rain.

The storm has passed and the aroma of recently showered flowers reaches your nose. The air around you is crisp and fresh. The rays of the sun have never seemed so bright and warm. The wet ground has now become dry and enjoyable, giving you reason to run and skip without any care. You hear the soft serenade of birds, a faint rustling of leaves, and the delicate sound of a nearby stream flowing along. You are free from fear and far from destruction. The path ahead of you has never looked so beautiful. It is in these times that you must not forget the one who brought you out of the storm. Do not forget the one who brought you such peace. Scripture promises us that He will never leave us, but we must also never leave Him.

It is easy to pray fervently when the storm rages, but it is harder to pray in the same way when everything is perfect. First Thessalonians 5:16-18 says, "Rejoice always, pray without ceasing, in everything give thanks; for this is the will of God in Christ Jesus for you." I encourage you to think of the sunshine as a time to recuperate. Use it as an opportunity to grow closer to God before you meet the next storm, rock pathway, or grassy overgrowth. Build up your defenses against temptation and trials so that you are ready when they come. Grow in your knowledge of God and the Bible so that you can apply it when the time comes. Finally, give thanks to God for bringing you out of those past encounters. Glorify Him alone because you did not make it through by yourself, but through His mercy and grace. Look up to your Father and thank Him for His sacrifice.

My Darling Daughter,

Now that you have decided to follow Me with all your heart, I cannot express to you all that I have in store for you. I have big plans for your life. If you would only trust Me, I will make them happen. You don't have to worry about anything, so stop worrying! The storms will pass, the grassy areas will clear, the rocky patch won't exist forever, and the sunny days will come and go. Through them all, always remember that I am here walking right beside you. There is no need for you to worry. You may be tempted to take matters into your own hands, but trust in the fact that I have everything under control.

I created the heavens and the earth; don't you think that I can control your life? If I can orchestrate the universe and the billions of lives on earth simultaneously, I can also fix the tiny problems of your life. I will help you with your research paper, your job placement, your college application, your house payment, and your relationships. I said in My Word that I will cover you with My feathers, and under My wings you may seek refuge; My faithfulness is a shield and bulwark" (Psalm 91:4). That which is a mountain to you is but a grain of sand to Me.

There is absolutely nothing to fear now that I'm here walking beside you. There is nothing left for you to worry about. I have it all in My hands; put your trust in Me and not in man (Psalm 118:8-9). The world will let you down, but I never will. Others will forsake you, but I will never leave your side. There are rough storms, sharper rocks, and even bigger overgrowths ahead, but I will lead you and protect you through them. Have faith and know that I am in control of everything. I will never hurt my daughter...I love you too much. I proved that to you on the cross (Romans 5:8).

Never forget that I know how it feels to be tempted (Matthew 4; Luke 4). There will always be rocks on your path, but do not walk on them. It is your responsibility to stay as far away from them as possible. If you do happen to walk upon them, remember that I am here to help you. When you fall, I will be there to pick you back up. It is not a sin to be tempted, but it is a sin to allow yourself to fall into that temptation. Stay with me and resist sin. I will never give you more than you can handle. I will always provide for you a door for escape from temptation. Choose to walk through that door (First Corinthians 10:13).

There is no one in the world stronger than I am. Be strong and courageous, and I will take care of the rest. Draw strength from the knowledge that I am in complete control. Have faith. Trust in Me with all your heart and do not rely on your understanding (Proverbs 3:5). I love you, My daughter. Remember always that you are a daughter of the Most High, the Almighty God. You are my beautiful little girl.

Your Heavenly Daddy

2

Becoming Daddy's Little Girl

Since Jesus died on the cross for our sins, He made it possible for us to inherit the riches of heaven (Ephesians 2:4-6). It is only because of Jesus' sacrifice that we are forgiven of all our sins (past, present, and future). He gave us the two greatest gifts of all time: His love and eternal life. Jesus also gave us grace, mercy, and the promise of heaven. He died that we might walk beside Him throughout our lives. He gave us the privilege to have fellowship with God the Father; we can speak to Him whenever we please. It is for these reasons that our perspectives must change toward how we view ourselves on our individual path.

In chapter one, I asked you to draw an imaginary picture of your path in your mind. Now I want you to erase it. Create an entirely new canvas. Turn the page, if you will. In this chapter, I want you to picture yourself not at the age and stature you are now, but rather as a child. A toddler, even. This may sound like a step backward and it certainly doesn't appeal to our natural desire for independence, but I ask you to do this for a very specific reason. No matter how old you get, it is important for you to remember that God is always your heavenly Father and you are His little girl.

You may be in high school, have your driver's license, moved out of your parents' house, gone away to college, or working full-time; nevertheless, you must always remember your need for Jesus to lead you down your path. The more you grow in your relationship with your heavenly Father, the more you will learn that growing spiritually has more to do with growing down, not up. When you allow God to increase in your life, you force your own self to decrease. You may be thinking, *How am I supposed to do that?* The answer is that your perspective desperately needs to be repaired.

Take the image of your path and your young self upon it, with God leading you down it. You are Daddy's little girl. You are humble and young, willing to both listen and learn. You are protected and loved by the one who created the universe. Picture yourself as a toddler who is just learning how to walk. Your legs are wobbly and uncoordinated; your arms are stretched out for balance. Though you are capable of walking on your own, your Father is standing right next to you walking. He is there for comfort and support, and to catch you if you start to fall. If you ask, He's there to carry you along when you get tired and to protect you when you're in danger.

The key to this entire mental picture is humility. In order for this to be your experience, you need to humble yourself before the Lord and the people around you (your parents, your boss, your teachers, your friends, etc.). This is not something that comes natural to us; it goes completely against our sinful nature. I speak from experience. It is a huge obstacle to humble yourself when your parents ask you to do the dishes, or when a teacher gives you an unnecessarily large amount of homework, but when we do we honor the Lord. It pleases Him when we submit to the authority He has placed over us. It makes our Father happy when we obey His commandments: "Children, obey your parents in all things, for this is well pleasing to the Lord" (Colossians 3:20).

To humble yourself means to cause yourself to decrease. James 4:6-7 says, "But He gives more grace. Therefore He says: 'God resists the proud, but gives grace to the humble.' Therefore submit to God. Resist the devil and he will flee from you." By submitting to God and not your own desires or feelings, you are humbling yourself. You're growing down. Instead of being prideful and trusting in your own strength, you rely on God and allow Him to increase in your life. Take on this posture of humility first of all because it is what your heavenly Father has commanded of you. However, when you humble yourself, God will also reward you. James 4:10 says, "Humble yourselves in the sight of the Lord, and He will lift you up." The fact that God allows you to call Him "Father" is a privilege. We thank Him for that special gift by being humble in all that we do.

God the Father is watching over you, Jesus is walking with you, and the Holy Spirit lives inside of you. This means that you are always in the presence of a King. If the Queen of England told you to clean your room, would you listen? If the President of the United States asked you to take out the trash, would you do it? It is imperative that we view God with the same respect, if not more. Colossians 3:17 tells us to "do all in the name of the Lord Jesus." When you don't feel like doing something that your parents or a teacher asks you to do, think about it as if Jesus Christ Himself were the one asking you. Replace those in earthly authority over you with the Lord. How different would you act if you changed your perspective in that way?

Mary, the mother of Jesus, had to make the decision of a lifetime; it is a decision that many of us would struggle to make today. She had to sacrifice her own plans and accept the plan that God made for her. Luke 1:26-38 describes an encounter Mary had with Gabriel, an angel of the Lord. The angel told her that though she was a virgin, she would give birth to a son whose name would be Jesus. He prophesied of the greatness and holiness of that child. At first, Mary was confused. She questioned the prophesy of Gabriel, wondering how she would be able to do so since she had never been intimate with a man. Eventually, however, Mary humbled herself to the will of God without complaint. She graciously accepted the opportunity to be the mother of Jesus, the man who would give Himself as a sacrifice for us. What an amazing opportunity! An incredible gift!

But what if the plan God has for you isn't as exciting as the plan He had for Mary? Should you still give up your plans in order to follow one that you're not certain about? Or even excited about? The answer is a resounding "yes!" God has bigger and better plans for you than you could ever have for yourself. He has plans that surpass even your wildest dreams. If you learn to be humble and to surrender your life to the one who created it, you will be blown away by the plan God created just for you.

As I stated in the previous chapter and attempted to make you picture in this chapter, your faith is represented by the image of yourself as a child. In Matthew 18, Jesus was asked by His disciples who would be the greatest in heaven? In verses 3-4, Jesus answered them, "Assuredly, I say to you, unless you are converted and become as little children, you will by no means enter the kingdom of heaven. Therefore whoever humbles himself as this little child is the greatest in the kingdom of heaven" (Matthew 18:3-4). When you spend time watching little children, you can't help but notice their innocent, joyful nature. They believe and trust with all their hearts, and those they trust they love unconditionally. Yet, they still depend on those they trust to feed, clothe, and nurture them. We need to have the same mentality when we view our relationship with God.

In order to be called "Daddy's little girl," we must first become little. We must depend, trust, and cling to our Father. We must love Him as He loves us—unconditionally. To be innocent like a child is a very hard feat; nevertheless, we should strive to be pure and blameless, to hate the things God hates, to love the things God loves, and to weep at the things that make God weep. We must keep our eyes from things that will lead us into temptation, our ears from things that are evil, and our tongues from speaking the evil we have heard.

We need to separate ourselves from the people and places that might cause us to compromise our childlike faith. We need to trust in the truth that when we obey the Lord's commandments, there will be great rewards on earth and in heaven. When we are tempted, we need to call out to God the Father to help us. Above all, we need to pray for the strength to do all of these things (Mark 14:38).

The key to having a close relationship with God is thirsting for one. Jesus demonstrated this for us in Mark 14:36. Right before He was arrested in the Garden of Gethsemane and beaten before a crowd, He cried out, "Abba, Father." Jesus lifted up a prayer, pleading with God to allow the burden to pass from Him. He addressed God in the same manner we are to address God, as a heavenly Father. Because Jesus died for us and now lives in us, we are enabled to address God in the same way. He accomplished this for us through His blood and death (Galatians 3:26-29, 4:6). It because of His sacrifice alone that we, as daughters, can call out to God the Father.

The relationship between a father and his daughter is a complex bond. While it is not easily understood, it is also not easily broken. But what happens when a father loves his daughter with all of his heart and the daughter only loves him with part of her heart? Such is often the case with God and His daughters. You may try to play it off like you love God in the same way He loves you, but do your actions prove it? Do you put Him at the bottom of your priority list, or the top? Do you choose to hang out with your non-believing friends first, or those from youth group? Do you ignore your parents when they ask you for a favor, or do you willingly serve them? These may seem like small things, but the reality is that it is the smallest things which affect our relationship with God. It is your heavenly Father's desire to see His little girl proving her love for Him in her everyday life, in both the big and the small moments. He wants to see His little girl falling in love with Him more and more every single day.

Any girl that has ever had a serious crush on a boy knows that he is all she can ever think about. You get butterflies every time you see him or his name is brought up in conversation. You pair together your first name with his last, just to see how it looks. You make a continuous effort to be around him. You do your hair differently one day just to see if he will notice. You always have your eyes on him, just in case he looks over at you. You start hanging around his friends so that you might get closer to him. You want to learn everything about him: his personality, his likes and dislikes, his hobbies, and basically anything that will give you the advantage to one day becoming his girlfriend. In short, you are head-over-heels for this boy.

One of the keys to becoming Daddy's little girl is to replace your crush with Jesus Christ. He should be the one you are always thinking about, the one you want to know absolutely everything about, and the one you always want to be in communication with. Fall in love with the one that fell in love with you first (1 John. 4:19). This is a prerequisite.

In order for you to be able to properly love someone on earth, you must love Jesus properly. The Bible tells us that we should first love God with our heart, mind, and soul, and then we should love our neighbors as ourselves (Matthew 22:37-40). We love God properly by doing our very best to please Him through obeying His Word. A manifestation of our true love for God is always a true love for His people.

The second key to becoming Daddy's little girl is recognizing His voice when He calls your name. There are many times when the voice of our Father will be calling out to us and we must know how to recognize it in order to respond. Mary Magdalene is taught this lesson in John 20 when she meets Jesus outside of His tomb. Jesus found her there and asked why she was weeping and who she was seeking. Mary Magdalene, however, didn't recognize the resurrected Christ, supposing Him to be the gardener. She began inquiring about Jesus' whereabouts, begging to know where He was so that she could take His body away. In verse 16, Jesus called the weeping woman to attention, saying, "Mary!" She immediately turned to Him and realized her mistake. Her response is what everyone's response should be when recognizing the voice of Christ; she called him "Rabboni," which can also be translated as teacher.

The reason Mary Magdalene was able to quickly identify Jesus was because she had spent a lot of her life around Him. The more acquainted you are with Jesus, the easier it becomes for you to pick out His voice from the crowd. The way you become acquainted with Jesus is by spending time in His Word, in prayer, and in fellowship with other believers who are following God's plan. When you let go of your selfish desires, you have more time to listen to God's desires for your life. God's voice is very distinct. It's that voice in your head that tells you to go talk to someone about Jesus. It's the voice of encouragement. Sometimes, it's even the voice of conviction.

Don't get God's voice mixed up with anyone else's. There are many competing voices in our ears—the voice of the world, and even the voice of the devil. It's those voices that will give you false hope and discourage you in your walk with God. The devil is always ready to find a crack in the foundation where he can squeeze in and wreak havoc. He's constantly looking for your mistakes so that he can capitalize on them. The Bible offers encouragement for our battle against the devil's demoralizing voice. Romans 8:1 says, "There is therefore now no condemnation to those who are in Christ Jesus, who do not walk according to the flesh, but according to the Spirit." Jesus took the condemnation that you deserved upon Himself when He went to the cross. God will never turn you away when you call on Him; you are His precious little girl. Because of that, you have nothing to be ashamed of. He nailed your imperfections and your failures to the cross.

Know your Father's voice. Be ready to hear even when you least expect to. Make sure you know Him well so that when His voice comes, you recognize it and are ready to receive what He has for you. If you are ever confused about whether or not you are hearing God's voice, ask one simple question. Does this agree or contradict with the Word of God? If it contradicts, it cannot be the voice of God. Become well acquainted with His voice by being well acquainted with the Bible. Your heavenly Father wants to speak to you; allow Him to talk and be willing to listen. Walk closer to Him so that He gets closer to you (James 4:8). Above all, keep your childlike faith.

Beloved,

You now know what it means to be My little girl. Now you can trust in the fact that I always take care of my daughters. However, being a daughter of the King is a big task. You must die to yourself and follow Me. You must humble yourself to everyone around you (your parents, teachers, bosses, friends, etc.). This is certainly hard, but by doing so, you're demonstrating your love for Me through obedience. It may be hard at times to keep your humility intact, but remember that you're doing so because I asked you to (Colossians 3:23). You're being humble for Me.

I don't want you to just say that you trust Me; I want you to prove it. There are times when I may test you, but these will be opportunities for you to let go of your own fears and rely on My strength. I always want what is best for my children; everything I do is for your good. I care about you more than the sparrows and lilies (Matthew 6:25-34). I will certainly provide for you. My Word says so.

Give Me your heart; I will take care of it better than you ever could. I know you better than you know yourself (Psalm 139:1). I am your Father and you are My child (1 John 3:1). Give your heart to Me because I will keep it safe. Fall in love with Me first before you try falling in love with anyone else. Wait for the man that I have planned for you; it will all be worth it if you only trust in My perfect timing for your life.

Because you are My daughter, it is important that you act like it. When you get dressed in the morning, remember that you are an ambassador of Me. Adorn yourself with the modesty befitting the daughter of the one true King. When you speak, remember that your words are a reflection of Me. When you struggle to represent Me well, ask for strength. You have the Holy Spirit within you; you have more power than you know (Acts 1:8).

If you ever feel lonely or scared, remember that I am here for you. I will never leave your side. Even though I cannot physically hold you, I am with you in Spirit and truth. You never need to ask whether or not I will stay. The real question is...will you stay with Me? Remember that apart from Me, you can do nothing, but with Me, you can do everything (John 15:5; Philippians 4:13). Please Me greatly with your love and obedience, and I will give you what you desire (Psalm 37:4).

I love you, My gorgeous daughter!

Your Heavenly Daddy

3

Holding Daddy's Hand

It's a beautiful day; the birds are singing wonderful melodies, the sun is bright and warm on your back, and you're walking side-by-side with Daddy. As you hold His hand, you feel a skip and lightness in your step. There's an unexpected dip in the path, but Daddy lifts you over it before you even have the chance to fall. A little later on, a fork appears in the road and you don't know which path to take. Fortunately, you don't need to know. As long as you are holding Daddy's hand, He will lead you in the correct way. The road may become a little dangerous. Every step is a cautious one, and you know that you could fall at any second, so you hold on to His hand tighter. He, too, knows the danger; He grips your hand tighter. The tighter your fingers are interlocked, the safer and more certain you feel. These are the benefits of walking with your Father and of being in fellowship with Him.

Often, when we think about communion, our minds immediately visualize bland crackers and grape juice. These elements are meant to represent Jesus' broken and bloodied body which hung on the cross for our sakes. Did you know, however, that communion can also be described as fellowship? When we walk down our life's path, side-by-side with the Lord, we are experiencing fellowship with Him. Just because you cannot physically see Him doesn't mean that you can't grow closer to Him. You can still learn more about Him, His likes and dislikes, His hopes and plans.

Believe it or not, God wants to be your best friend. He wants to be the one you keep secrets with, the one you confide in, the one you talk to all the time. When you have a bad day, He wants you to turn to Him with the heavy weight of it all. You don't need to be afraid of dumping all your problems on the Lord because that's exactly what He wants you to do (Psalm 55:22; 1 Peter 5:7).

Being best friends with God is a big commitment. James 4:4 is clear, "Adulterers and adulteresses! Do you not know that friendship with the world is enmity with God? Whoever therefore wants to be a friend of the world makes himself an enemy of God." A decision must be made: will you befriend God or will you befriend the world? If you are a self-proclaimed Christian and friend of God, then there are things you have to lay aside, such as partying, listening to perverse music, and associating closely with non-believers. Once you make the decision to follow the Lord, you can no longer associate yourself with the world. You must rely fully on your Father to lead and protect you. The comforting thing is this: He will never stop catching you when you fall. He will never get frustrated with you reaching out to Him. He is fully committed to His relationship with you.

A third meaning of communion is conversation. Prayer is the easiest way for us to have a conversation with our Father. The greatest benefit is that we can pray whenever we want, wherever we want. Prayer is not confined to a certain time or location. Because God is with us wherever we go, we are allowed to pray wherever we go. First Thessalonians 5:17 tells us, "Pray without ceasing." Our communion with God through prayer should never stop. It needs to be a habit, a fundamental part of our everyday lives. Just as we should never let go of our Father's hand, we must never stop talking to Him either.

When a small child is just learning how to talk, it seems like their parents can't get them to stop. They talk about anything and everything that pops into their little heads. The way we talk to Jesus should be no different. We should tell Him every feeling, emotion, and desire. We should give Him every single feeling, positive or negative. Our prayer life should never cease. Not only should we be in constant communication with God, but we should also set aside a very specific amount of time each day that we focus on nothing other than talking to Him. It could be right when you wake up in the morning, right before you fall asleep at night, or anytime in between. Whatever works best for you, stick to it. Don't let anything intrude upon that quality time with your Father.

In Daniel 5, King Belshazzar of Babylon was killed and Darius the Mede took over the Babylonian kingdom. At that point, Daniel had found favor in the sight of King Darius, so the king set Daniel as one of three governors in charge of the kingdom. When the other governors and princes of the kingdom heard this news, they set out to find fault in Daniel and jeopardize any claim he may have to the throne in the future. After failing to find a justifiable fault, the governors and princes convinced King Darius to write a decree: anyone who prayed to any god or man (other than to King Darius) over the following thirty days, would be thrown into a den of lions. Daniel's response was this: "Now when Daniel knew that the writing was signed, he went home. And in his upper room, with his windows open toward Jerusalem, he knelt down on his knees three times that day, and prayed and gave thanks before his God, as was his custom since early days" (Daniel 6:10).

Daniel was not moved by what he knew was coming. He was fully aware that if he continued to pray, he would be caught and thrown into a den of lions. However, he did not compromise in his faith; he prayed three times a day to the one true God. He kept his priorities in check and knew that God would protect him. No consequence could dissuade Daniel from worshiping God. At the end of the chapter, Daniel was arrested and thrown into the lions' den. His death was imminent, but God had other plans. When the King returned to the den the next day to check on Daniel, he was astonished by the fact that Daniel was still alive! God had put a hold on the lions' mouths in order to protect His faithful son (Daniel 6:20-23).

Our faith needs to be like that of Daniel's. There are so many times in life when we come across a small bump in the road and our tendency is to panic. We fail to remember that God will always take care of those who remain faithful to Him. Instead of panicking, we need to turn to God in faithful prayer. James 1:6 says, "But let him ask in faith, with no doubting, for he who doubts is like a wave of the sea driven and tossed by the wind." Instead of being rattled by our fear, we need to stand firm in the faithfulness and protection of our Father. When you are scared or doubting, turn to Him to supply all that you need. Turn to Him in unrivaled prayer and worship.

When we pray to God in a time of need, we must remember that we are *asking* Him for something, not telling Him to do something. Further, it would be foolish of us to automatically assume that He will give us all that we ask. God always reserves the right to give or deny us of what we seek. Our attitude toward prayer should always be, first and foremost, for God's will to be done. We can certainly make our requests known to God, but prior to doing so there are a few questions we should ask ourselves. First, why are you praying for that particular area? Second, what are your motives behind that prayer? If you ask the Lord for something, but your heart is not in the right place, do not be surprised when the Lord doesn't fulfill that request. James 4:3 says, "You ask and do not receive, because you ask amiss, that you may spend it on your pleasures."

Are you praying that your unsaved boyfriend will come to know Jesus because you want to take your relationship one step further? Or because you want to see his life changed for the glory of God? Are you going on a missions trip to take some cool pictures and have something cool to talk about? Or because you want to share the beautiful news of the gospel with those who have never heard it before? Turn your eyes inside out. Examine your own heart. The main motivation for everything you do should always be Jesus-centered. The fulfillment of His will should be your desire. When you ask God for something, ask in Jesus' name so that He can be glorified (John 14:13-14).

Don't let anything come between your communication with your heavenly Father. Daniel prayed in faith three times a day and no thing or person would keep him from doing so. That is your personal time with God to communicate, rejuvenate, and heal. Decide when you will spend that time with God and do everything in your power to keep that appointment. Time spent with God is time that will never go to waste.

When you go before the Lord in prayer with anger, sin, or an unclean heart, that prayer will go unheard. Scripture is abundantly clear: "If I regard iniquity in my heart, the Lord will not hear" (Psalm 66:18). When you come to God with a request, your heart must be free from sin. Even though you have been forgiven of your sins by the blood of Jesus, you must still ask for forgiveness when you sin. Any time you enter into the throne room of God, you must do so with a clean heart. You must have forgiven those who have done you wrong and no longer live in contempt. You must not be holding on to any grudges. Forgive those that have done you wrong, because God forgave you for what you've done Him wrong (Luke 17:3-4). Come to God with a heart that has been cleansed and ask that you may be forgiven for any sin known or unknown, so that God will not be hindered when He hears your prayer.

Here is a list of some more verses on prayer that you can study on your own: Psalm 34:15, 17-18; Psalm 116:17; Proverbs 15:8; Matthew 6:5-6, 9-13; Matthew 7:7-8; Matthew 21:22; Mark 11:24-25; John 15:7; Ephesians 6:18; Philippians 4:6; First Thessalonians 5:17; First Timothy 2:1; and James 5:13.

Holding Daddy's hand demonstrates your dependence upon Him; it shows that you trust the Lord to lead and guide you in the right direction. Choosing to hold His hand is always the first step, but the real challenge comes in continuing to hold on to Him. Acknowledging the importance of prayer and communion with your Father is level one. Remaining dependent upon Him is level two. The latter is more difficult because it requires a daily decision, a steadfastness that goes against our very nature as humans. We want independence, we want to be self-sufficient, we don't want to seem weak.

Depending on God requires you to abide in Him. An illustration given in scripture is that of a branch. A branch cannot survive on its own; it needs to be connected to the vine. In John 15, Jesus called Himself the true vine that bears all fruitful branches. These branches represent the body of Christ, and the individual stems the faithful Christians. The purpose of a branch is to bear fruit, which is only made possible by remaining connected to the vine. Jesus declared, "I am the vine, you are the branches. He who abides in Me, and I in him, bears much fruit; for without Me you can do nothing" (John 15:5). Without the vine, the branches are powerless, worthless. That's the same idea as you with Jesus—you need Him.

What does the Bible mean by "bearing fruit"? It first may be helpful for you to consider the purpose of fruit. Fruit is a source of food and nourishment. The metaphorical fruit that comes from your life should be visible; it should give others spiritual nourishment and strength. It should encourage them to bear fruit of their own. So what kind of fruit are you producing? Sweet and nourishing fruit? Or bitter and rotten fruit? If the motives behind your actions are bitter and rotten, so will be your fruit. But if your motivation comes from pursuing the will of God for your life, your fruit will be sweet and nourishing. Galatians 5:22-23 lists nine different fruits that you should be producing as a branch connected to the one true vine: "But the fruit of the Spirit is love, joy, peace, longsuffering, kindness, goodness, faithfulness, gentleness, self-control. Against such there is no law."

When you abide in God, you're depending on Him to give you the essentials and the ability needed to bear fruit. This is your responsibility as a Christian. If a branch doesn't bear fruit, it is cut off from the vine. If there is no evidence of your faith, you will be as a branch tossed into the fire (John 15:6). Don't let your faith go to waste by not putting it to good use. Tell people about the good news of the gospel, practice the commandments laid out in scripture, love your enemies, and help those in need. There are so many ways to activate your faith. When you do these things with pure motives, you will bear fruit. When others observe you glorifying God in such practical ways, they will be nourished by the fruit you bear.

As you continue down your path with your focus fixed on God's will and remaining dependent upon Him, you may still encounter some unexpected potholes or speed bumps. As long as you keep on holding His hand, you have the assurance that He will not let you fall. The day you let go is the day you will trip and crash to the ground in pain. Stay steadfast; be mindful to abide in Him always. Proverbs 3:5-6 says, "Trust in the Lord with all your heart, and lean not on your own understanding; in all your ways acknowledge Him, and He shall direct your paths." The Father has a much different understanding of the path ahead than you do. Where you see danger and fear, God sees an opportunity to shape His beloved daughter into the woman He desires her to be. He sees the storms ahead as a time for you two to grow closer to one another as you depend on Him to carry you through it. Trust in His wisdom and strength, not in your own.

When I was five years old, my dad decided to teach me how to rollerblade. He thought the best way was to start in our one-car garage. It was just big enough for me to skate in circles and get used to the feeling. He put the skates on me and helped me up, but I couldn't even stand by myself without falling. He came up with the idea to wrap a thick, winter scarf around my waist. He kept a grip on the other end so that if I lost my balance and started to fall, he could easily pull me back up before I hit the floor. It worked every time! I had more confidence to learn because I knew that my dad wouldn't let me fall. I trusted him to pull me back up. I could clumsily skate around without fear because I knew he was going to protect me.

How much more so should we trust in the protection of our heavenly Father? Knowing that we can hold His hand should be the biggest source of comfort in our lives. More than anyone else, the Lord will protect us. Who better to place our trust in than the King of Kings and Lord of Lords? He has remained faithful to take care of us in the past, in the present, and will continue to do so in the future (2 Samuel 22:3).

Depending upon and trusting in God will inevitably reap safety and direction for you as you continue down your path. When you depend and trust in Him, He will protect you from danger, but if you doubt His power, you will lose sight of Jesus. If you pray in disbelief and doubt that God can deliver you, you might as well have asked for a scarecrow to protect you. Psalm 91:4 gives you the comfort that God will "cover you with His feathers, and under His wings you shall take refuge; His truth shall be your shield and buckler." You have a personal bodyguard named Jesus who is with you wherever you go. He knows the danger ahead and wants to prepare you for the trial so you are ready when it comes. He wants you to lean on Him to carry you through it. You are completely safe with Him, so stay with Him! Psalm 27:1 says, "The Lord is my light and my salvation; whom shall I fear? The Lord is the strength of my life; of whom shall I be afraid?" You don't need to fear anyone or anything when you have God on your side. With Him, you can take on any situation that appears on your path.

In First Samuel 17, a little shepherd boy named David went up against Goliath, a giant in the Philistine army. Yet, David had no fear because God was on his side. He had full confidence, not in his own strength, but in the strength of the Lord. David knew that God had protected him in the past and would continue to do so in the future. As the famous story goes, David took five smooth stones with him out onto the battlefield. First Samuel 17:48-49 recounts the underdog story, "So it was, when the Philistine arose and came and drew near to meet David, that David hurried and ran toward the army to meet the Philistine. Then David put his hand in his bag and took out a stone; and he slung it and struck the Philistine in his forehead, so that the stone sank into his forehead, and he fell on his face to the earth." I want you to notice that David didn't chicken out right before he was supposed to fight Goliath. He actually *ran* up to the front line to meet the giant. He had a great faith and boldness in this moment because of his dependence upon God. We should meet our own life's trials with the same perspective and countenance.

Hanging out with Jesus and keeping your prayer appointments are the two ways to hold your heavenly Father's hand. The benefits of holding His hand come after you realize that you need to depend on and trust in Him to take care of you. When you trust Him, He gives you safety. An important benefit that you receive from trusting the Lord is direction for your life. When you make it a habit to be in constant communication with your Father, you have someone who always knows where to go. You do not have complete control over your own path, but you can hold on to the one who does. He knows every bump, rock, grassy patch, turn, and exit ahead. He knows every highway, detour, and side street. Hold on to His hand, trust in Him, and He will keep you safe and give you direction.

Cherished One,

My desire for you is to be close to Me. I want to hear your voice just as much as you want to hear Mine. If you ever think that I'm not listening to you…think again! I always want to talk to you. I don't care how small or insignificant your requests may be; I want to be included in everything. Please communicate with Me as often as you can. Remember what I wrote in First Thessalonians 5:17, "Pray without ceasing." Your prayer life shouldn't be a hassle, but a joy.

It should be something you desire to do. Whenever you feel alone or lost, I hope that your first instinct is to turn to Me. I'm never far away, and I'm always waiting for you.

Don't let go of My hand. I don't enjoy watching you stumble or fall. If you do let go of My hand, the only thing I can do for you is dust you off and kiss away the pain. But if you never let go, I can protect you better. I will hold you tighter than anyone else can. My hands created the sun and the stars, the elephants and the whales, the universe and the galaxies, yet they are just small enough to hold your hand.

My beautiful daughter, I created you to have fellowship with Me. I love it when you give Me all your cares and worries. Nothing is ever too big or too small. When I say nothing, I mean absolutely NOTHING. Please remember to hold My hand. Put your life in the palm of My hands because I am more than qualified to protect you. You are so precious to Me and holding your hand allows Me to be closer to you. It also allows Me to take charge and lead you the way I want to. I promise you I will never lead you astray. I love you so much (1 John 4:10).

Your Heavenly Daddy

4

Daddy, Carry Me

You and your Daddy have been walking for some time now. You have learned to humble yourself. You understand how to hold His hand. Once in a while, you encounter grassy areas or rocky patches, but you haven't let go of Him.

Eventually, the excitement you had when you first learned you are Daddy's little princess starts fading away. You no longer have the energy to play and dance around with your Daddy. You're tired of the same old, same old…there's nothing new anymore. Suddenly, something unexpected pops up and startles you. You're terrified of all the unknown problems and difficulties you didn't see coming. Your path begins to darken. A storm is coming and it seems more frightening than any of the rocky patches you've encountered before. For some reason, you've allowed fear to cripple you. You don't even have the strength to walk anymore. There's nowhere to run or hide. Fear engulfs you. The thought of walking one step further makes you sick.

When you first became Daddy's little girl, everything was new and exciting. Every star was an unexplained phenomenon, and every flower was a miracle. At first, you were having such a wonderful time watching God work in your life. Getting an "A" on a test was an enormous feat. Finding a five-dollar bill in your pocket was grounds for a massive celebration. Getting the chance to witness to someone and share the gospel was an extraordinary event.

Yet, after walking with God for some time, you notice your passion for Him has started to fade. All of the flowers start to smell the same, the stars are just lights in the sky, and the exciting animals are now boring decorations. You're tired of walking; your feet are tired, your legs are wobbly, your heart is weary, and you've lost the energy to go on.

How did it come to this? Before you were so happy and excited to walk with God. Now you're bored and looking for ways to occupy yourself. Jesus was once your everything, but now He just doesn't seem to be enough. He is no longer the center of your world. Church has become a routine instead of a craving. Reading God's Word has evolved into a duty instead of a passion. Praying is now a ritual, not an honor. Your boredom with God has caused those things, which you previously made a priority, to fall to the bottom of the list.

As a result, the trials that you once viewed as an occasion to perfect your faith are now vicious hurricanes destroying your heart. Storm after storm, trial after trial, wave after wave, your path is constantly bombarded by impairments you no longer have the strength to deal with.

Don't feel discouraged if you're in this valley. You're not the only one to ever feel this way; there comes a time when every Christ-follower feels weary and drained. If holding your Daddy's hand is not enough to comfort you anymore, then ask Him to carry you. The Lord will not carry you against your will; He wants you to admit that you are weak and need Him. The great thing about God is that He can turn your weakness into His strength. Satan uses thorns and hindrances as weapons to cripple you, but God uses them as tools to mold you.

In Second Corinthians 12, Paul writes about his personal experience with weakness. He tells the church in Corinth, "A thorn in the flesh was given to me, a messenger of Satan to buffet me, lest I be exalted above measure. Concerning this thing I pleaded with the Lord three times that it might depart from me. And He said to me, 'My grace is sufficient for you, for My strength is made perfect in weakness.' Therefore most gladly I will rather boast in my infirmities, that the power of Christ may rest upon me" (2 Corinthians 12:7-9). Paul is showing his audience that God can use a weakness and turn it into a strength. What you view as a crippling disability can be transformed by God into a victorious talent. God will accomplish this amazing transformation when you give up trying to do it yourself.

Don't trick yourself into thinking that you can resolve problems on your own. You cannot transform your weaknesses into strengths just by working hard enough. The point Paul makes in Second Corinthians 12 is that only God is capable of doing that. Stop trying to do things in your own power. Turn over your struggles to God and trust that He wants to transform them for His glory.

The key is to not view your weaknesses as imperfections, but as a chance to take a break from walking. It's a chance for you to rest in your Father's arms. In God's eyes, your weariness is His opportunity to humble you and strengthen His Spirit within you. When you readily admit you need His help, He will gladly come to your rescue and give you rest. You have no power to change your circumstances without receiving help from the one true King. Without Jesus, you can do nothing, but with Jesus, you can do anything (Philippians 4:13).

Some situations in your life may be unbearable. School projects, boy troubles, peer pressure, issues with friends, loneliness, humiliation, instruction from your parents, and even an unexpected quiz can rock your world. Everyone thinks you're blowing it all out of proportion, telling you things like "You're such a drama queen!" and "Get a grip!" Your friends don't understand and your parents have no idea what you're going through, but Jesus does. He lived, bled, and died as a man. He understands abandonment and humiliation. He emptied Himself in order to relate to you (Philippians 2:7). He put His immortality on hold so you could call out to Him and He would understand you. You are never alone; Jesus is "with you always, even to the end of the age" (Matthew 28:20).

Asking your Daddy to carry you doesn't just mean you're tired and want a break. It also means you've asked Him to handle all your drama. Cast your cares on Jesus because He cares about you (1 Peter 5:7). Stop trying to fix it on your own. The greatest thing about giving all your problems to Jesus is that He won't leave anything left for you to worry about. Giving everything to Him gives you an opportunity to find true rest in His arms. No one else can ever comfort you the way He can. No one else can ever provide for you the way He can. Rest in Him. He is more than able to handle whatever mountain you are facing.

Have you ever seen a parent carrying their sleeping child in their arms? The child's mouth is wide open and drool drips onto the parent's shirt. Small arms and legs sway lifelessly as the parent walks. The child is able to sleep so soundly because they have complete confidence in the one holding them. They know that their mom or dad won't drop them. You must have the same trust concerning being in your Daddy's arms. Close your eyes and let go of whatever you're holding on to so tightly. Find rest in His arms, building up energy for the road ahead. He won't ever drop you.

You suddenly find yourself in the midst of a storm. Your circumstances have grown into something overwhelming. Every little thing scares you. Your grades are slipping, you find out that a close family member has cancer, you can't figure out what you're going to do once you graduate. The storm starts out as a small shower, but it quickly turns into a terrifying hurricane. You've never been so scared in your whole life as much as you are right now.

When these times come, it is important you don't let the storm take over your life. Run to your Daddy's open arms.

He's waiting patiently for you to realize the storm is too big for you to handle on your own. He's waiting for you to realize you need Him to handle it for you. You can boast and brag about your heavenly Father because nothing is too big for Him to handle. He's braver than any bodyguard, tougher than any Navy SEAL, and stronger than any weightlifter. Don't run away from Him. Let Him take care of you.

Walking on your path is sometimes frightening. Unexpected things pop up and startle you. A normal day to one person might be an unrelenting storm to you. Being afraid is normal. You're not any less of a person for admitting you're afraid. The good news is that Jesus has conquered all these things! He has overcome humiliation, temptation, betrayal, physical and mental injury, and loneliness. He has even conquered death!

Here are some verses to show you just how much your Daddy has overcome: Matthew 4:1-11; Matthew 27:29-30; Matthew 28:6; Mark 16:6; Luke 4:1-13; Luke 22:47-48, 63-65; Luke 23:11, 21-22; Luke 24:6; 1 Corinthians 15:55-57.

Jesus knows what it's like to be betrayed by someone close to you. He knows what it's like to be made fun of by a crowd. As Jesus was beaten and whipped, the surrounding crowd mocked and scorned His name. Jesus could've easily pulled the plug on His Father's plan, but He knew He had to finish the task set before Him. He could've allowed the angels to wreak havoc on the crowd, but He showed mercy and grace to those watching. He could have smoked the soldiers that were whipping Him and made ashes of the nails they drove through His hands and feet, but He didn't. He bore all the pain and abuse and, in the end, He had victory over all those things. Jesus says in John 16:33, "These things I have spoken to you, that in Me you may have peace. In the world you will have tribulation; but be of good cheer, I have overcome the world."

Jesus is your refuge and strong tower. No one can do a better job than Him. Proverbs 18:10 says, "The name of the Lord is a strong tower; the righteous run to it and are safe." If you are ever feeling scared or unsure, ask Him to carry you. Speak the words of Psalm 91 to your heart, "I will say of the Lord, 'He is my refuge and my fortress; my God, in Him I will trust'…He shall cover you with His feathers, and under His wings you shall take refuge; His truth shall be your shield and buckler" (Psalm 91:2, 4).

A child might ask their mom or dad to carry them for a couple of reasons. The obvious ones are because they're either afraid or tired. However, there's one other reason that hasn't been mentioned yet. Sometimes a child asks their parents to hold them because they want a sense of comfort and closeness. You don't just have to ask your Daddy to carry you when you're scared or exhausted. You can ask to be carried when you desire to be closer to Jesus. If you draw near to God, He will draw near to you (James 4:8). He always wants to hold you. The question is, do you want to be held?

Your path is unpredictable; situations come up without warning and catch you off guard. They can throw you into a completely different direction. The unpredictability of your path may eventually lead to fear, weariness, and fatigue, but when those times come around, don't give up on Jesus. Stay dependent on Him and He will carry you through whatever problems arise. Most importantly, don't make it a habit of just being carried when you're scared or tired. Make a commitment to ask to be carried even when things are going great. You need to draw closer to your Daddy in the light and carefree times just as much as you do in the dark and scary times.

When tragedy and hardship come your way, you will be tempted to think your world is falling apart and that God is far from you. Instead of looking at your problems as mountains that cannot be climbed, look at them as tests. Are you going to run away from God's arms or are you going to run into God's arms?

You are a daughter of the one true King. The same Spirit that raised people from the dead and healed the sick lives in you. The same Spirit that propelled David to face Goliath lives in you. The same Spirit that gave Mary the courage to take on the task of bearing the Savior of the world lives in you. As you look to humble yourself before the Lord, grow in the knowledge that you have been given a spirit of power, love, and self-control (2 Timothy 1:7).

Now that you've asked your Daddy to carry you, rest and enjoy the closeness of His presence. Rest in the understanding that you need His comfort and strength. Find rejuvenation in His arms. Once you are ready, stand on your own two feet with boldness and renewed strength. Get ready to face all those situations you've been battling with regained power. The fear that previously paralyzed you is now acknowledged and relinquished. Rejoice in the weaknesses that once hindered you, trusting God to accomplish His will. Only He can transform those weaknesses into strengths.

Stand with boldness in your faith and who God has made you. Walk in confidence, knowing you are made in His image. Look ahead to your future with courage! No matter what you face, your Daddy will be right there waiting, ready for you to call out and lift up your arms to Him.

My Precious Daughter,

What a beautiful young lady you are becoming! I am so proud of you and what you are making of your life! You are very special to Me. I uniquely created you to be this way; you are the only one like you on this earth. I know being a teenager can be tough, especially when other girls your age are doing things and dressing in certain ways to get guys to notice them. I know you feel like you need to fit in, but remember that I have a great plan for you! I promise you will feel beautiful and happy if you accept who I made you to be.

One day, there will be a special, godly young man who will see the wonderful person you are. He will desire you for all the right reasons. Please don't feel like you have to give in to the pressures around you just because other girls are getting more attention. Don't let anyone convince you that your virginity doesn't matter. Your purity and godliness will be greatly rewarded. One day, you will look back on this time in your life and be thankful you didn't compromise. Keep holding My hand and reaching your arms out to Me, and I will never let you down.

Your Heavenly Daddy

5

The Boy in the Sandbox

Your encounters up until now have been challenging; you've gone through all of nature's furies and have remained by your Daddy's side. As you continue to walk with Him, you spot a boy off to the side of your path.

You don't just glance at him…you stop and stare. You start noticing many things about him. He's about your age and he's really cute. He's playing in a sandbox with all the same things you like to play with. He wears the same kind of clothes you wear. He's even looking over at you right now! Your eyes and his eyes connect, and you feel nervous and excited all at the same time. He stops what he's doing and stands up. Then he invites you to come play with him. You're reluctant at first, but he's so cute and nice, and he's even offering to share his toys with you.

You jump off your path to go play with him, leaving your Daddy behind. In time, you forget about your Daddy altogether. He's trying to get your attention, but you're too busy with your new friend to notice. You're afraid that if you don't give the little boy your full attention, he'll kick you out of his sandbox. You don't feel bad about spending all your time with him because there are so many other little girls playing in different sandboxes with other little boys.

As time goes on, playing is not enough for the little boy you've dedicated all your time to. He wants more from you. He wants to know if you're committed to staying with him and if you're serious about your relationship with him. He asks you to compromise your beliefs to prove your commitment. You give in…now what?

Earlier in the book, I wrote about the rocks and all the other dangerous things that can appear on your path. Well, the little boy in the sandbox is also one of those things. He is a representation of the temptation that wants to tear you away from your Daddy. How should you handle this temptation?

There have always been these temptations in your life. There's the boy in your geometry class, the boy who lives next door, and the boy who unexpectedly steals your eye when you're out with your friends. You don't know if you should date any of them because they're not believers. You snap back to reality; you're holding Daddy's hand! However, that doesn't stop the argument going on in your head.

"He's so cute!"

"But I can't…"

"You don't understand; I like him a lot! I really want to go out with him!"

It may not seem like this situation is detrimental to you, but the truth is, you're being distracted. The enemy wants to pull you as far as he can away from your Daddy. He wants to use your feelings to lead you into a situation that will be difficult to get out of. You know you're in trouble, but you still want to play with the boy in the sandbox. It doesn't matter that he's not walking with Jesus. It's your biggest desire to be with him. That's when you finally realize you're being tempted.

When someone surrenders their life to Jesus, they are usually on fire for Him; they can't contain all the good news building up inside. The same thing happens when someone returns from a church retreat or camp. It's these moments that the enemy sees as a prime opportunity to attack. He wants to take you out. What he sends your way isn't a little league toss…it's a major league curveball.

It sounds pretty pessimistic to say when you're on a spiritual high that you're bound to be attacked and thrown off track. When Jesus miraculously fed the five thousand, it was a time of awe and celebration. Afterward, he went away into the wilderness…to be tempted. How did He stand firm while being vigorously tempted for 40 days and nights?

As a Christian, your strongest weapon against the enemy's temptations is the Word of God. It is the strongest line of defense you have when you are being led away from your Daddy's side. In the wilderness, Jesus fought against Satan's temptations with the Bible. Every attack the devil sent His way was deflected with God's Word (Matthew 4:1-11).

The sandbox attempts to pull you away from your Daddy's side, but you know deep down that those thoughts and feelings are wrong—God's Word has spoken against them. The sandbox tells you to explore your sexuality and that you get to decide what is right. The sandbox tells you God is withholding good things from you and doesn't want you to have fun. The sandbox says the Bible is too rigid and prevents you from being truly free. What the sandbox doesn't tell you is that a lot of pain will come from leaving your Daddy's side.

God's Word shows you how to stay next to your heavenly Father. It offers guidelines that will benefit you when you obey them. The Bible says not to have any other gods before the Lord because they will leave you empty. You are supposed to honor your parents because they only want what's best for you. Don't steal because it will hurt your neighbors. Stop coveting because comparison and envy will only bring you down. God's commandments are always there for your benefit.

Religion says, "Do this or else."

Jesus says, "Do this and live well."

When you obey God's commandments, you will find satisfaction and peace in Him. There is a great value in God's Word in that it illuminates the path you need to walk down.

Whether or not you commit to walking down that path is up to you. God will not force you down it.

There will always be boys in sandboxes wherever you go. They will tempt you to lust and compromise your beliefs. You must stop yourself before your feelings get too far. Fall back on God's Word. If you fall into temptation, don't think God has given up on you. He will never get tired of picking you up when you fall! Open your Bible and set your mind on Jesus. Divert your attention away from the little boy in the sandbox and fix your attention on your Daddy.

God will never give you more than you can handle. First Corinthians 10:13 says, "No temptation has overtaken you except such as is common to man; but God is faithful, who will not allow you to be tempted beyond what you are able, but with the temptation will also make the way of escape, that you may be able to bear it." Not only will He not give you more than you can handle, but He will also give you an escape route from that temptation. God always provides an open door for you to walk through so you can get away from a bad situation.

You can't fight your selfish desires on your own. There is a war waging inside of you between God's spirit and your sinful nature. When you realize you're being tempted by something, you must pray. Ask God to give you the strength you need to battle your flesh so that you can overcome temptation and stay faithful to Him.

Maybe your friends, peers, and those on social media are pressuring you to get a boyfriend. Maybe you feel like a loser because everyone else is dating someone and you're not. After some time, you start asking, "What's wrong with me? Why don't I have a boyfriend?" It seems like every show you watch on TV revolves around dating. You can't escape it. You end up compromising your faith by going out with the first guy that thinks you're cute and takes an interest in you. He's not God's best for you, but you didn't wait.

Don't listen to other people. Don't believe what those on social media are saying. The only opinion you should care about is your Daddy's. Second Corinthians 6:17 says, "Come out from among them and be separate, says the Lord. Do not touch what is unclean, and I will receive you." Being different for Jesus' sake is better than being the same as everyone else and getting hurt. When you jump into a relationship just for the sake of being in one, you will get hurt! It's only a matter of time. Just because you don't have a boyfriend doesn't mean you're worthless. It just means you have more time to focus on what God wants you to do.

The desire to fit in and belong to a group engulfs everyone. You want to be a part of the crowd and blend in with society. You want to be up to speed with all the latest fashion trends. You want to look like the girls on Pinterest and Instagram. At what point is the pursuit of changing your look destroying the person God made you to be? At what point is it detrimental to your walk with Christ?

Dressing a certain way may attract more attention, but that doesn't mean it's the right kind of attention. If you claim to be a Christian, yet you dress inappropriately, you are ruining your witness. People should know you are a disciple of Jesus by the way you dress, act, and talk. Instead of worrying so much about what other people think about you, consider what God thinks. When you wake up in the morning and get dressed, look in the mirror and pretend Jesus is in the room with you (truthfully, He is!). Try to see yourself through your Daddy's eyes instead.

He looks at you and sees the most beautiful creation ever. He created you so uniquely—with every curve and color. He created you with a unique personality and a personalized heartbeat. Once you accept that God created you with a specific intention and purpose, you'll find confidence in what you look like. If you're not comfortable with the colors God gave you, you will never learn to spread your wings and be who He created you to be.

You've conquered temptation and peer pressure, but you still feel lonely. You vow to not compromise your beliefs again, but you still find yourself wanting. What you desire is companionship, and that desire makes the boy in the sandbox look even more tempting. You think you'll be happy if you go play with him. After all, Genesis 2:18 says that it's not good for a person to be alone, right? You mistake God's Word for a green light to go back to the sandbox with the little boy, leaving your Daddy behind. The little boy is able to temporarily fill the void in your heart, but he will never be able to protect you from the storm that is coming. Your Daddy is the only one who can do that. When the little boy abandons you in the storm completely, you're forced to run back to your Daddy for help. He's waiting for you, but you had to learn the hard way.

Don't miss out on Mr. Right because you settled for Mr. Right Now! When God created you, He had your future husband in mind; when God created your future husband, He had you in mind. He has the right guy out there for you…your job is to wait! The point of waiting is not to make you suffer, but to protect you from those who are not right for you. Trust that God has the perfect man for you! Trust that He will bring him when it is the right time! Trust that His plan for marriage is better than the world's!

The world says sex before marriage isn't a big deal, but God's Word says otherwise. Hebrews 13:4 says, "Marriage is honorable among all, and the bed undefiled; but fornicators and adulterers God will judge." Compromising your purity grieves your Daddy, but staying pure brings Him honor. Marriage is something that must be taken seriously, and sex even more so. Don't miss out on God's best for you by falling into the trap of the world's lies. Trust Him!

When you're feeling lonely, turn to Jesus. When you start struggling with overwhelming desires for companionship and intimacy, give it all to your Daddy. Depend on Him for support, comfort, and friendship. A relationship with Him is more important than any earthly relationship anyway. In time, He will bring along Mr. Right!

If you've compromised your beliefs and fallen into temptation, don't give up. Jesus is always waiting for you to run back to Him. It's never too late to ask for forgiveness.

[74]

The best thing about your Daddy is that He will never turn you away. He'll never get tired of picking you up when you fall. He'll never refuse to heal you! Second Corinthians 5:17 says, "Therefore, if anyone is in Christ, he is a new creation; old things have passed away; behold, all things have become new." Don't compromise the new life God has given you by turning back to your old ways.

No matter what you do, whether you give in to temptation, peer pressure, or loneliness, whether you go to the boy in the sandbox or not, your Daddy is always waiting for you back on the path He carved for you. He's waiting patiently for you to realize the boy in the sandbox is not the one He has made for you. No matter what, your Daddy will never get tired of you. He will never let you go. You are His beautiful little girl; don't let anyone tell you otherwise!

6

Don't Let Go

The boy in the sandbox was quite the trial. What else could arise that would put a strain on your relationship with your Daddy?

As you're walking, you notice there aren't just sandboxes off the road. There are other little girls just like you…and they have lemonade stands. It seems like they're making a lot of money from selling lemonade, which they spend on new toys and expensive clothes. Not only are there lemonade stands, but there are also other little girls playing with different little boys on jungle gyms, swings, and seesaws. The little girls aren't just playing with one little boy either; they're playing with every little boy they see.

One little girl in particular catches your eye. She is wearing incredibly tight clothes that show off her extremely skinny figure. You think it is impossible to ever look as good as she does. You also notice she doesn't eat a lot…just enough to keep herself alive.

Another little girl walks by. She's drinking a lot of punch and eating a lot of candy. It's not the candy you're used to. It makes her super skinny and gets her really hyper. She can't stop herself from eating it. She has to steal and beg for more when she runs out. Her whole life revolves around it.

Suddenly, a million flashes of light blind you. Click! Click! Click! There's so many people taking pictures of another girl. She must be insanely popular. She doesn't just have money. She doesn't just play with all the boys. She doesn't just have a perfect body and expensive clothes. She has it all! Everybody knows her name. Everybody is dying to take a picture with her.

These girls look like they're having so much fun! You know they have hard things happen every once in a while, but for the most part, they seem happy. You want to learn how to get what they have…maybe even more. Before you know it, you're living among the crowd and putting everything aside to achieve your goals. All you care about is money, fame, and beauty. How did it get this far?

It is so easy to get caught up in the world's definition of happiness. According to the world, happiness comes from having a perfect body or a lot of money. The world says you will only be happy when you fight to achieve your goals, not caring if you hurt other people along the way. The world tries to convince you that happiness will come from a relationship or from having sex. You are under constant bombardment with these false realities.

You can fend off the world's lies by remembering your Daddy and His Word. When you talk to Him, He is able to strengthen you to overcome the world's temptations. When you make Him the biggest priority of your life, the rest will inevitably fall into place. That doesn't mean hard things won't happen, but it does mean your heavenly Daddy will be there to help you through them. No matter what stage of life you're in, don't let your goals consume you. Don't let them replace the time you should be dedicating to your Daddy. School, jobs, relationships...nothing should ever take His place as the main priority of your life.

You could be the busiest person on the face of the planet, but you still need to make time for God. He has the entire universe to manage, yet He still makes time for you. Psalm 139:17-18 says, "How precious also are Your thoughts to me, O God! How great is the sum of them! If I should count them, they would be more in number than the sand; when I awake, I am still with You." When you go to the beach, you can never escape the millions of grains of sand that are around you. Sand gets in your clothes, hair, car...it even follows you home! That's how many thoughts God has for you! How amazing is that?

The world doesn't understand how profitable it is to be in communication with God. Time spent at church, in prayer, and in communion is seen as wasted time. However, Matthew 16:26 offers the sobering truth, "For what profit is it to a man if he gains the whole world, and loses his own soul? Or what will a man give in exchange for his soul?" You could be the smartest, wealthiest, and most successful person on the face of the earth, but if you don't have a relationship with Jesus, none of it matters.

Sometimes, it may seem like having a lot of money makes everything better. At times, yes, life seems a lot easier when you have cash to spend. It gives you the security of knowing you can feed yourself, clothe yourself, put gas in your car, and keep a roof over your head. However, money should never be the focal point of your life. Placing an overemphasis on money can be very dangerous. First Timothy 6:10 says, "For the love of money is a root of all kinds of evil, for which some have strayed from the faith in their greediness, and pierced themselves through with many sorrows." You cannot buy joy. You can't use your credit card to get healing. You can't write a check and purchase love. Only God can provide these things for you.

So far you've learned to not put work and school before Jesus. You've learned that a love of money will destroy you. Now you're facing an image issue. It bothers you that your body doesn't match the actresses on TV. It bothers you that you can't fit into a size 3. It bothers you that your chest is too small, or that you have a chubby face and fat thighs. You've tried everything to fix your appearance, but nothing seems to work. Every single picture reminds you of your imperfections. All you think about is how other people view you.

God doesn't make mistakes. He formed you perfectly. You don't need validation from others to feel confident in the way you look. The Bible says, "For the Lord does not see as man sees; for man looks at the outward appearance, but the Lord looks at the heart" (1 Samuel 16:7). There is nothing wrong with dressing up and looking nice, but don't let that be your focus. Focus your energy on beautifying your inside, not your outside. Work on producing fruit, giving your time to Jesus, and loving others the best you can. Work on your heart by resisting temptation and placing all of your trust in your Daddy. He doesn't care about how cute your shoes are or how you choose to do your hair in the morning. He cares more about how well you treat others and obey His commandments.

Within the comfort of your Daddy's arms, another boy catches your eye. The sandbox he is playing in looks way more fun than the last one. He seems so nice. His friends are funny and great to be around. Not only is he nicer than the last little boy, but he's way cuter too! You can't take your eyes off him. Would it be so wrong for you to go play with him? Yes! The Bible says, "Whoever looks at a woman to lust for her has already committed adultery with her in his heart" (Matthew 5:28). Don't think this verse lets you off the hook because it is addressed to the boys; it applies to girls as well. An earthly relationship should never take the place of the one you have with your heavenly Father.

To let go of your Daddy's hand and join the little boy in his sandbox would be to forsake your heavenly Father. It doesn't just end with playing either! Soon you're spending all your time with him and his friends. You start drinking and using inappropriate language. You start lying and gossiping. You start watching bad movies and listening to vulgar music again. You've dug yourself into a hole so deep that you can hardly see the way out anymore. You let go of your Daddy's hand and have drifted the furthest you've ever been away from Him.

Jeremiah 15:6 reads, "'You have forsaken Me,' says the Lord, 'You have gone backward. Therefore I will stretch out My hand against you and destroy you; I am weary of relenting!'" God hates sin, but He still loves you. He sent His only Son to earth to die for all your sins. That doesn't mean you're off the hook and have been given a free ticket to sin all you want. Jesus isn't some sort of insurance plan. He isn't some new toy that you buy and then forget about in a couple weeks. He isn't someone that gets placed at the bottom of the priority list. Jesus created the heavens and the earth. He created you with a specific, beautiful, and unique design. Don't let go of His hand for a world that will leave you empty and broken.

John 10:10 says, "The thief does not come except to steal, and to kill, and to destroy. I [Jesus] have come that they may have life, and that they may have it more abundantly." The world will make you feel like you're missing out on something—relationships, money, fame, fun. The world will tempt you to leave your Daddy in hopes of something better. However, there is nothing better than holding His hand. There is nothing better than being directed by Him down the path He carved specifically for you.

When you fall down, He will pick you up. He will brush the dirt off your knees and wipe the tears off your cheeks. He will hold you as you cry. He will remind you that He loves you and will never leave you. He will forgive you for your shortcomings and show you the way to everlasting life. No matter what, He will always be waiting for you to return to Him.

Cling to your Daddy and don't let go!

7

Patience, Little One

Your wounds are healed. You've been given a second chance by your Daddy. You start out walking with your Daddy again slowly, aware of the trials and temptations that will inevitably come your way. He holds your hand and you cling to Him tighter than ever before. The storms are more bearable with your Daddy at your side to protect you. The rocky areas are not as tempting as before. The grassy overgrowths are no longer a threat. You don't even look twice at the sandboxes on the side of the path. You have a Daddy who died for you and would do anything to protect you. The love He offers you is more precious than anything that little boy in the sandbox could offer you. With all that in mind, you press on with confidence.

After some time, you realize Mr. Right is nowhere in sight. The boys in the sandboxes are definitely not your future husband...so where is he? Why hasn't he swept you off your feet yet? You're growing impatient. You're still holding Daddy's hand, but you're not giving Him your full attention. Your thoughts are consumed with your future husband. Who is he? Where is he? When will he finally show up? Eventually, you start questioning God's intentions, doubting that He has anyone picked out for you at all. Frustrated and confused, you let go of your Daddy's hand and throw yourself to the floor. You start pounding your hands and feet against the pavement.

Let's face the facts...there are times when you throw tantrums and it's not pretty. You get impatient and start losing your trust in God. You start to believe He's not who He says He is. You want to meet your future husband now, but God won't bring him to you. The truth is the problem is not with God, it's with you. Isaiah 40:31 says, "Those who wait on the Lord shall renew their strength; they shall mount up with wings like eagles, they shall run and not be weary, they shall walk and not faint." Trust in His timing, not your own. You may think you're ready for your future husband to show up, but God knows better.

You need to learn patience. The apostle Paul lists patience as the very first characteristic in his definition of love in First Corinthians 13. In Galatians 5:22, he lists patience as one of the fruits of the Spirit. According to the Oxford English Dictionary, patience is described as "perseverance; ability to endure; forbearance." No one ever said waiting is easy. It is really hard to be patient for something—especially something you can't see. That waiting period God has you in is the perfect time to get closer to Him, learn more about Him, and fall deeper in love with Him.

Stop looking around at everybody else. Look up toward heaven. Colossians 3:2 says, "Set your mind on things above, not on things on the earth." When you keep your mind fixed on heaven, you won't be bogged down by the things of earth. You can't keep any of those things anyway. When you die, you leave behind your clothes, possessions, phone, car, and even your closest relationships. Jesus told the rich young ruler in Matthew 19:21, "If you want to be perfect, go, sell what you have and give to the poor, and you will have treasure in heaven; and come, follow Me." Everything you need is in Christ. Don't ever let your mind wander away from what is most important.

You might be tempted at times to close your eyes because they feel heavy and tired. Don't do it! Keep your full attention on Jesus, even when you're weary. Fix your eyes on Jesus even when the world tells you to look at something else. No matter what the circumstance, don't stop seeking after His face. It will always be a challenge to have patience in seasons when God calls you to wait. You might be tempted to chase after momentary gratification when it seems like God is withholding something from you. Keep pressing on; He will fulfill the desires of your heart in His perfect timing!

If you don't remember anything else from this chapter, remember this: when you learn that your eyes were made for looking at Jesus, you will discover a surprise that will sweep you off your feet! Keep your eyes on Him!

8

Daddy, Who is He?

The thought of your future husband occupies your mind from time to time; however, as time passes, you realize the best place to be is in the arms of your Daddy. After enduring many trials, you know that Jesus is all you need. Though the storms don't cease completely, you're at peace. Rocky patches appear from time to time, and sometimes the grass gets thick, but you've learned your lesson. All you have to do is keep holding your Daddy's hand.

Instead of fixing your eyes on what you don't have, you've switched your perspective to focus on what you do have. Once again, you find yourself in awe of the beauty of the path your Daddy has carved for you. You notice how brightly the sun shines down on you. The flowers, trees, mountains, streams, and animals are beautiful reminders of the one holding your hand. All you want to do is spend as much time with Him as possible. He picks you up and twirls you around. Your arms are stretched out, enjoying the sensation of the wind floating through your hair. Laughter spills from your lips. You're the happiest you've ever been.

As you wait on the desires of your heart to come to fruition, focus on drawing near to your heavenly Father.

When you are close to Him, the agony of waiting will be no more. Just because the right guy hasn't come into your life yet doesn't mean you should give up on God. Everything is completely under His control. Romans 8:28 says, "And we know that all things work together for good to those who love God, to those who are the called according to His purpose." Everything will work out as it should; just be patient!

Don't get discouraged. Don't give up the fight. Keep praying to your Daddy for the strength to get through each day. Pray that you would find complete contentment in His arms. The Bible says, "Be anxious for nothing, but in everything by prayer and supplication, with thanksgiving, let your requests be made known to God; and the peace of God, which surpasses all understanding, will guard your hearts and minds through Christ Jesus" (Philippians 4:6-7).

After you tell your Daddy what you want, stop dwelling on it. Stop constantly wondering when Mr. Right is going to show up. Use that time to pray. On the nights when you feel lonely, give your tears to your Daddy. God will "supply all your need according to His riches in glory by Christ Jesus" (Philippians 4:19). He will give you what you need when you need it. He knows exactly when and where you will meet your future husband. Keep your attention on Him; you won't regret it!

Your little feet push forward as you walk along your path. You've stayed next to your Father faithfully for a while now. Your tiny hand has not let go of His strong one. Your chin is tilted upward and your eyes are focused on the face of Jesus. Slowly, He reveals His other arm. You realize He is holding another tiny hand. It belongs to a handsome little boy.

You ask, "Daddy, who is he?"

God doesn't need to say anything. In time, you figure out that the little boy is your future husband.

There are two main differences between the little boy God has prepared for you to marry and the boy in the sandbox. First, your future husband is holding your Daddy's hand. The little boy in the sandbox never wanted to hold God's hand; he ignored God completely. Second, the little boy holding your Daddy's hand isn't a distraction. He causes you to look at Jesus, not away from Him. A good indication you've met Mr. Right is that he builds you up instead of knocking you down. He doesn't throw sand in your face. He is strong in the areas you are weak. He is everything you need and more.

Notice I said "need," not "want." Your Daddy knows exactly what you need and don't need. God knows you better than you know yourself, and He knows your husband better than he knows himself. He had your relationship planned before either of you were born. God wove you together while you were in your mother's womb (Psalm 139:13). He spent nine months forming everything about you: your personality, likes and dislikes, hair color, and skin tone. He gave you qualities that would separate you from the rest of the world. He created you with all the characteristics that would complete the missing parts of your future husband.

There are a lot of solid Christian guys out there that will cause you to look at Jesus, but you need to consider the qualities you need. You need someone you are attracted to, someone who will match your intellectual state, someone who is strong where you are weak, and someone who builds you up spiritually. It is also important that you marry a man who believes in the same Jesus you do. He needs to hold on to your Daddy's hand with the same amount of faith and trust as you do.

Saying you are a believer is one thing, but proving it is completely different. Have you seen fruit in his life? Have you witnessed him keep his faith through life's trials? Does he encourage you to have a better relationship with Jesus? Second Corinthians 6:14 warns, "Do not be unequally yoked together with unbelievers. For what fellowship has righteousness with lawlessness? And what communion has light with darkness?" The man who makes going to church, reading his Bible, and praying every day a priority will most likely have a good relationship with Jesus. That's the man you want to marry.

Ultimately, the relationship you have with Jesus will determine the relationship you have with your future husband. Keep Jesus as the King of your life and He will bring you Prince Charming when it is time. When your husband comes along, don't elevate him over your heavenly Father. God is the only one who can heal your bumps and bruises. He is the only one who can protect you in the storm. He is the only one who can give you peace and contentment.

If you dethrone your Daddy for a mere human, you'll be in trouble!

When you find your Prince Charming, include God in your conversations and activities. Make sure the things you're doing together would be approved by Him. If you have to think twice about something, you probably shouldn't do it. Set healthy, God-honoring boundaries and stick to them. Don't put yourself in a situation that could jeopardize your purity. Fix your eyes on Him together and He will keep you from falling into sin.

Sometimes, staying focused on Jesus when you meet Prince Charming is difficult. You just love him so much! You've been dreaming about him for years! However, including God in the situation will always be worth it. When you and your husband are fighting, when one of you loses your job, or when you're having a hard time paying the bills, Jesus will be your comfort. When you stay in the castle the one true King prepared for you, you will be protected when the enemy invades. The day you take Him out of the equation is the day things start crumbling. Make sure you are both holding His hand.

With all this talk about your future husband, you must be excited to meet him already. Whatever you do, don't peek! You're dying to know who he is and when he will come, but you have to be patient. Stop trying to guess if you already know him. Stop wondering if every Christian guy you talk to is him. Find contentment in having your Daddy…He is more than enough. The more you try to peek, the longer you'll have to wait. Wait for the one God has planned for you. In the meantime, rest in His presence.

Paul says "if we hope for what we do not see, we eagerly wait for it with perseverance" (Romans 8:25). Once you find complete contentment and absolute satisfaction in the presence of God, you will find rest. The matters of your future husband are in God's hands. Have faith that Jesus will bring you a man that will love Him more than he loves you. Until then, draw closer to God so you will be able to discern when the right guy comes along. Don't settle for Mr. Right Now just because you're feeling lonely or because all of your friends have boyfriends. There is the perfect man out there for you. He is holding on to your Daddy's other hand; you will see him when your heavenly Father says it is time.

Choose Jesus even when the world thinks you're being insensible. Keep your eyes fixed on Jesus when your path gets grassy, when you come across a fork in the road, and when you see a boy in a sandbox. Keep your eyes on Jesus when the devil tempts you and when the world calls out your name. Cling to Him when you see a storm on the horizon. Hold His hand even when you want to let go. Lift your arms up to Him when you are too weary to keep going. Run to Him if you ever drift away. Don't forget His promises. Your Daddy only wants what is best for His daughters.

Be patient and wait.

Acknowledgments

A special thanks to Erik Sahakian who has been called to establish Abundant Harvest Publishing and to call out authors to speak. Without his help and dedication, this book would still be on a hard drive and not on printed paper. Thank you and your team for bringing this book to life.

To my sister, who, no matter the challenge, has stood up and supported me. To my best friend, who wouldn't let me forget about this book and reminded me to get moving!

I'd like to give another special thanks to my husband, Tristan, and my mom. When this was just a burning in my heart, my mom supported me to pursue writing. And when it came to bringing this book into the world, my husband stood up and pushed it forward.

About the Author

Natalie Jones has committed to sharing her journey of purity and pursues a platform to express its importance with all young women. She currently resides in Savannah, GA with her husband and new baby.